Alexandria, Virginia

Where History Lives

By Craig Lancto

Alexandria, Virginia:
Where History Lives

Craig Lancto

Good Gnus Press
CCI Press, Alexandra, VA

Published by **Good Gnus Press**, a subsidiary of
CCI Press
Alexandria, VA 22301
www.goodgnuspress.com

Copyright © 2008 by Craig Lancto
All rights reserved

Cover image: Gadby's Tavern by Craig Lancto

Manufactured in the United States

ISBN-978-0-9826749-0-1

Library of Congress Cataloging-in-Publication Data

Lancto, Craig
Alexandria, Virginia: Where History Lives
An illustrated walking tour of historic Alexandria, Virginia.

Includes images and index of sites

Abridged for exclusive use of the
Near East South Asia Center for Strategic Studies.

Contents

Where the Book Takes You

This book is divided into two sections. The first is the core walking tour, which takes about an hour at a brisk walk. It begins at the Torpedo Factory on the Potomac River, goes two blocks west on King to the Ramsay House, and turns north for a block past Carlyle House and Alexandria Bank before turning west again at Wise's Tavern on Cameron, passing City Hall, Gadsby's Tavern and the Fairfax-Yeaton house before running into Christ's Church on Washington Street.

Continuing west through the Christ Church graveyard to Columbus Street, it turns south for a block to King Street, where the trolley service offers a chance to run up to the George Washington Memorial Temple. (Even with good timing, a quick visit to the temple will double to the original hour set aside for a quick tour.) If time does not permit, it offers a quick look at the majestic building while walking another block west to Alfred Street, where a turn south leads past Friendship Fire House to Prince Street at the end of the block.

Turning east on Prince Street the walk continues to the Appomattox (Confederate Soldier) Statue at the intersection of Prince and South Washington streets.

At the statue, it jogs south a block past the Lyceum and turns left on Duke Street where it passes between the Dulaney house on the left and the Lafayette house on the right at the intersection of South Saint Asaph Street.

Continuing east on Duke for another block, it turns north at South Pitt Street and turns east on King Street, where a plaque commemorates the Marshall House deaths of Colonel Ellsworth and James Jackson first fatalities of the Civil War and continues east past Market Square to the intersection of South Fairfax, where it stops at the Stabler-Leadbeater Apothecary Museum, within sight of the Ramsay House Visitors Center and close to many excellent restaurants.

The section that follows Stabler-Leadbeater includes other sites of interest as time allows.

The free King Street Trolley shuttles from the Potomac to the King Street subway stop — stopping every other block — about every 30 minutes.

The Freedom House Slave Museum is about two blocks south of King Street. A few blocks farther south on West Street leaves you in a cemetery. When you reach the east-west road in the cemetery, the gates to the west mark the original Alexandria National (Soldiers) Cemetery.

Liberty's Womb

If Boston is the "Cradle of Liberty,"
then Alexandria must be its womb.

As important as Boston was to the Revolution, Alexandria distills history into an eight-block matrix of history. One would be hard-pressed to find anyone of note in either the American revolution or the War Between the States who did not walk King or Cameron streets between Lee (once Water) and Washington streets.

Today this beautifully restored city pays homage to its heritage in historic sites and re-enactments with an overlay of arts and fine dining.

The intent of this book is to present a plan to visit some of the main sites, with enough information about them to make the visit interesting and to make the most of a brief stay.

A nimble visitor should be able to complete the circuit in an hour, but stopping in to visit each of the sites open to the public could easily fill a day.

Alexandria is not a city that should be rushed. For a thoroughly modern city, it remains remarkably quaint and friendly. Whether you choose to try one of the wonderful restaurants or to stop to catch your breath at one of the dozens of parks or in market square, take the time to enjoy one of America's greatest treasures.

Despite having lived here for more than three decades, I continue to be surprised by some bit of history I had overlooked.

I hope that I can convey even a modicum of the pleasure and excitement I experience every time I walk through Alexandria.

The Stabler-Leadbeater Apothecary

Torpedo Factory Art Gallery

www.torpedofactory.org
105 North Union Street

My favorite way to arrive in Alexandria ...

...is by boat.

...For most of us, that means a water taxi from National Harbor, just across the Potomac to the southeast, or from Georgetown, a few miles up river.

Coming by boat allows a good view of Old Town and the parks that line the river. It also means debarking at the city docks at the bottom of Cameron Street, and a perfect opportunity to visit the Torpedo Factory Art Studio at 105 North Union Street.

The Torpedo Factory, at left above, stands at the northeast corner of the intersection of King and Union streets.

When Alexandria was young, Union Street was mud flats and shallows (and the Potomac still reclaims its wetlands during heavy floods).

The attractive two-story building houses six galleries, the Art School of Alexandria and 160 artists who work, exhibit, and sell their art out of more than 80 studios. The Alexandria Archaeology Museum (http://oha.alexandriava.gov/archaeology) on the second floor offers exhibits about Alexandria's history, hands-on activities and excellent tours of Alexandria sites of interest. All free.

In November of 1918 the U.S. Navy began constructing the U.S. Naval Torpedo Station, for the manufacture and maintenance of torpedoes. After about five years it was converted to a munitions depot until the outbreak of World War II.

The bright green 9920 MK torpedo displayed in the main hall, a gift from the Navy Seabees, was manufactured here in 1945 . Its color was designed to help find it during testing. The silver aircraft torpedo near the exit at the rear of the building was built elsewhere.

Torpedo Factory

During the second world war, nearly 6,000 workers kept the plant operating around the clock manufacturing Mark XIV torpedoes for submarines and Mark IIIs for aircraft.

At war's end in June of 1945 the building was used as storage space for government documents, German war films and records, and objects from the Smithsonian Institution.

Alexandria bought the massive complex that included this building from the federal government in 1969. Local artist Marian Van Landingham led a movement to create an art center in the structure. The Torpedo Factory Art Center opened September 15, 1974.

In 1982 -1983, the artists moved to a temporary location while the city gutted and renovated the building as part of a plan to develop the waterfront. A second floor and two staircases were added at the same time, and the building was reopened on May 20, 1983.

Now attracting an estimated 8,000 visitors a year, the Torpedo Factory hosts changing exhibits and monthly Second Thursday Arts Night events. The Arts Center has become the anchor of a dynamic arts community in Alexandria, contributing to the city's frequently being named as one of the top arts destinations in the United States.

If the weather is good, especially on weekends, you might encounter special activities on the docks behind the Torpedo Factory.

Tickets for the water taxi and boat tours, including to the Mount Vernon estate, are available for purchase at the Potomoac Riverboat Company's kiosk on the docks.

As you leave the Torpedo Factory, walk south to the corner of King and Union streets, where you have a fine view of the colonial streetscape and the George Washington Masonic Temple at the top of King. The Ramsay House Visitor's Center is on the north side of King Street, about two blocks west.

The paddle wheeler Cherry Blossom, at right, is a popular venue for events.

Ramsay House

221 King Street   http://visitalexandriava.com

*R*estored by the City of Alexandria in 1956, Ramsay House originally was the home of William Ramsay, Scottish merchant, one of Alexandra's founders (1749), its first mayor and a close friend of George Washington-- who apparently never slept here. City historians believe that Ramsay built the house in Dumphries in 1724 and had the house barged up-river to its present site, which at the time, would have been on a steep rise overlooking the Potomac. Since then the wetlands have been filled in.

The people at the information desk are friendly and eager to help you enjoy your stay in Alexandria.

Ramsay House staff report seeing a peculiar man in colonial garb after dark. (We do not believe that they mean a walking tour guide.)

When your dogs are barking, let them chase cars...Trolley cars

*F*our free red trolleys operate from 10 a.m. to 10 p.m., seven days a week, so one should come by about every thirty minutes. The trolleys stop at signed stops about two blocks apart, from the bottom of King Street near the river to the Metrorail station, near the Masonic Temple.

Streetwise Orientation

The Old Town section of Alexandria was laid out in a neat grid system. Unlike many older towns that grew like Topsy, Alexandria is orderly and organized.

The Potomac River runs roughly north-south, so the parallel streets—Union, Lee, Fairfax, Royal, Pitt, St. Asaph, and Washington (also known as the Mount Vernon Parkway—also run north and south. Union Street seems to be an obvious nod to the Yankee invaders—Sorry, the Federal Troops—that occupied the city from May 1861 through the months after it ended in 1865. Other streets honor leading colonial families.

St. Asaph Street is less obvious than some of the others. It was named in honor of Jonathan Shipley, the Anglican Bishop of St. Asaph Cathedral in Wales and a supporter of American independence.

Continuing west, the streets are named after other notables, including Revolutionary leaders. Route I north, for example, is Patrick Street, Route I south is Henry. A U-turn from the south allows a traveler to follow Patrick-Henry, which explains the rush hour plaint heard from literate, trapped drivers, to "Give me liberty, or give me death."

The east-west streets in the center of town are named to honor royalty in descending order of importance, males to the south. So, traveling south from King, one crosses Prince and then Duke streets. Moving north crosses Cameron, (probably slipped in to honor Lord Fairfax, Baron of Cameron, who lived on the street) Queen and Princess.

Beyond the core streets, the names are less logical. Duke, for example is followed by Wolfe, in honor of the British general's defeating French General Montcalm on the Plains of Abraham near Quebec in 1759, effectively winning the French and Indian Wars. Moving north, past Princess, comes Oronoco Street, named for a type of tobacco. Alexandria's first tobacco warehouses, were at West's Point at the foot of this street, now, the site of Robinson Terminal, where the *Washington Post* stores tons of newsprint.

Market Square

300 Block of King Street

$\mathcal{M}$arket Square is the site of one of the (if not the) oldest continual farmer's markets in the country. (Saturday mornings year-round, from 5 a.m. – 10 a.m.)

$\mathcal{A}$cross N. Fairfax Street from Ramsay House, the tranquil square with the graceful fountains has been the scene of political and military activity for well over 200 years.

This was the site of the Fairfax Town Hall and Courthouse built in 1752, where George Mason and other local leaders wrote The Fairfax County Resolves in 1774. A precursor of the Declaration of Independence, the Fairfax Resolves or Resolutions demanded fair treatment for colonists.

Here, George Washington drilled the Virginia militia as district adjutant in 1754; General Braddock's troops drilled here as well.

In the mid nineteenth century, Market Square was the site of slave auctions .

Today the square hosts political gatherings, concerts, and other events throughout the year.

SITE OF
ASSEMBLY HALL
HERE WAS HELD MARCH 22 1785 THE FIRST CONFERENCE BETWEEN REPRESENTATIVES ALEXANDER HENDERSON AND GEORGE MASON OF VIRGINIA AND MAJOR DANIEL OF ST. THOMAS JENIFER, Mr. CHASE AND Mr. STONE OF MARYLAND. THIS CONFERENCE RESULTED IN THE FRAMING OF THE CONSTITUTION OF THE UNITED STATES.
ERECTED BY THE
ALEXANDRIA CHAMBER OF COMMERCE

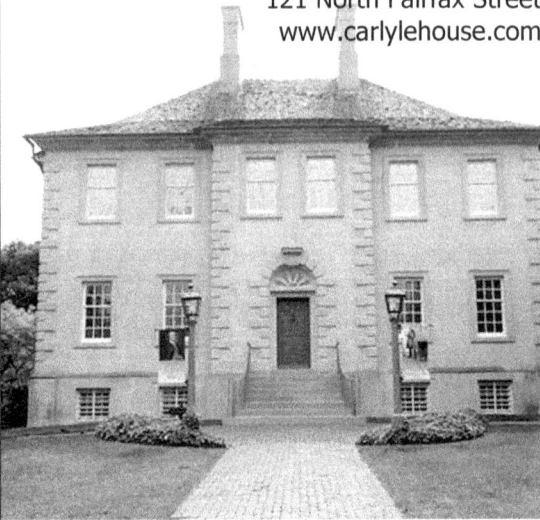

Carlyle House

121 North Fairfax Street
www.carlylehouse.com

Death Comes to Carlyle House

The historic house presents an exhibit on the mourning practices of 18th century Virginia, with the house itself draped in mourning. On Oct. 29, an 18th century funeral will be re-enacted 6-10 p.m., with a replica of a coffin and a deathbed scene. On that night, Alexandria's "Footsteps to the Past" ghost tour begins at the house and ends at John Carlyle's grave.

Exhibit included in regular admission price. Additional cost for the re-enactment and the re-enactment with a ghost tour of Old Town.

Tue-Sat 10-4

Check with Ramsay House (page 10) for current information.

The uncommon stone Georgian Palladian country house completed in 1753 is a testament to the wealth and standing of merchant and customs inspector John Carlyle, who designed and built this house for his marriage to Sarah Fairfax. (George Washington's half-brother, Lawrence Washington, was married to Ann Fairfax, Sarah's sister.)

General Edward Braddock, British Commander-in-Chief during the French and Indian War, was headquartered here. He met in the "Blue Room" with the royal governors of Virginia, Massachusetts, Maryland, Pennsylvania, and New York to discuss funding the French and Indian War.

Colonial Army Lieutenant George Washington, who attended the meeting, opposed General Braddock's plan for the Indian campaign -- in which Braddock died. Washington led the troops' retreat... And presided over Braddock's burial.

In another meeting Washington attended here, the governors of Maryland and Virginia determined the boundary between the two colonies.

The Bank of Alexandria

N. Fairfax and Cameron

The Alexandria Bank building next to the Carlyle House was the second purpose-built bank in America. Now a private business, during the War Between the States, the building was part of the rambling James Green Mansion House complex that was the city's largest hospital for sick and wounded soldiers.

Wise's Tavern

201 N. Fairfax at Cameron Street

Directly across Cameron Street, also on the east side, is the building that was known as Wise's (after owner James Wise, who also owned the better-known Gadsby's) Tavern in the 18th century.

Here, George Washington danced at a ball to celebrate ratification of the Constittution in 1788 and at birthday balls in his honor in 1792 and 1794.

It was in this building that George Washington was first called the "president' of the United States.

City Hall
300 Block of King/Cameron Street

From the beginning of Alexandria's existence, the founders planned to have the town hall and market square on the site it still occupies on the 300 block of King Street (the main entrance is on the Cameron street side).

The earliest town hall and court house was built on this site in 1752. The current building was erected in 1871. The brick building, once formed a 'U' around a central courtyard containing market sheds. Arhitect Adolph Kluss designed the Second French Empire building to look like the one that had burned in 1871, with Baroque detailing and several different types of three-dimensional massing. The clock tower is a replica of one designed by Benjamin Latrobe for an earlier town hall built in 1817 and destroyed by fire in 1871.

George Washington was Master of the Masonic Lodge that adjoined the original city hall. Some of the contents of the lodge, of which General Washington was Master, are now arranged in the Replica Room at the Masonic Temple, that soaring tower you probably saw when you were looking west on King Street.

(More about that later, under the **George Washington Masonic National Memorial**, page 22 AND 23.)

On July 18, 1774, George Washington and George Mason met with other county residents at the Fairfax Courthouse on Market Square (current site of City Hall) to approve the Fairfax Resolves. (Continued on next page.)

City Hall (cont.)

These resolutions (written by Mason) asserted the colonists' rights under British law and called for actions including a congress of representatives from each colony to prepare a plan for the "Defence and preservation of our Common rights" and a boycott of all English goods. City Hall also serves as an art gallery. If you have time to take a look, the second floor is lined with the work of local artists; the exhibition changes twice a year.

City Hall also boasts a rotating art exhibition, both in its corridors and in the mayors conference room. Walk west on Cameron Street, noting the memorial plaques that give further information about City Hall. At the end of the block, look across the street to see the famed Gadsby's Tavern.

Gadsby's Tavern & City Hotel

134 North Royal Street   www.gadsbytavern.org

Gadsby's Tavern today includes two buildings, the 1785 Georgian tavern and 1792 City Hotel, both of which have been restored to their 18th century condition. Today the buildings are named for Englishman John Gadsby who operated them from 1796 to 1806.

It also has been known as the City Tavern, Wise's Tavern, Sign of the Bunch of Grapes and Gadsby's Hotel.

Through most of the 19th century, it was simply the City Hotel

The two buildings of Gadsby's Tavern provide a side-by-side comparison of Georgian and Federal architecture. The smaller, south building, built around 1770, is Georgian. The larger 1792 Federal-style building has a much plainer façade.

Used as a tavern and hotel into the late 19th century, the buildings went through a variety of commercial uses before falling into disrepair. When the American Legion Post 24 purchased the buildings in 1929, they returned to the Gadsby's Tavern designation. The buildings were given to the City of Alexandria, restored, and reopened for the 1976 Bicentennial celebration.

Gadsby's Tavern

*A*s the largest 18th century gathering place in Alexandria, Gadsby's hosted dances, theatrical and musical performances and meetings of local organizations.

After he was president, Washington attended the first two birthnight celebrations in his honor at Gadsby's. The tradition continues today--without the General.

General Washington reviewed his troops for the last time from these steps.

Gadsby's Tavern has hosted most notables from the Revolutionary era. George Washington used Gadsby's as his headquarters when he was colonial of Virginia's colonial militia and again when he joined General Braddock's staff. His troops drilled across the street in Market Square.

Also among its frequent guests, Gadsby's numbers John Adams, Thomas Jefferson, James Madison, James Monroe, John Paul Jones and the Marquis de LaFayette.

Today, visitors can dine at Gadsbys or tour the historic rooms of both buildings, restored to their eighteenth century appearance. Visitors may tour the buildings during the day or during some of the special celebrations such as the annual Candlelight Tour in December, a particularly charming event with mulled cider and madrigals.

Gadsby's offers demonstrations and lessons of colonial pastimes, throughout the year, including sword-fighting and period dancing. While some rooms appear to await returning colonial diners, Gadsby's offers modern diners some colonial favorites as well as some updated fare.

Gadsby's Ice Well

On the sidewalk at the corner of Cameron and Royal, notice the ring of dark bricks that marks the boundary of the brick-lined ice well that Mr. Wise added around 1793. One of the few ice wells still in existence, this well, just over 17 feet wide and almost 12 feet deep, held close to 70 tons of ice. It was accessible from the street or by way of a brick-lined tunnel from the basement.

A viewing area accessible by stairs from the street was added in 1976.

Learn more and see some excellent photos at
http://gadsbys.home.att.net/ice well.htm

Fairfax-Yeaton House
607 Cameron Street

Around 1800, William Yeaton, who also designed George Washington's tomb and the Alexandria Academy, (Page 39) built this beautiful home, residence of Thomas, ninth Lord Fairfax, Baron Cameron and his son, Dr. Orlando Fairfax, until 1875. (Be sure to peek into the lovely garden to the right.)

Narrowest House in America

523 Queen Street

*J*ohn Hollensbury was tired of the neighbors' carriage wheels grinding against the wall of his house when they entered the alley next door, so the brick-maker bought the space out of spite and filled it with a house for his daughters. The interior walls of the seven-foot wide house, which *Ripley's Believe It or Not* once identified as the narrowest house in America -- believe it or not-- still show the marks left by carriage wheels on the exterior walls of the adjoining houses. At 36 feet deep, the two-story house, which the current owners use as a pied-a-terre when they visit Old Town, requires the careful use of available space.

Potomac Riverboat Company

Arriving from Georgetown or National Harbor

*A*n increasing number of visitors are approaching Alexandria from the water, whether from Georgetown or by water taxi from National Harbor. Either way, they will most likely be aboard one of the Potomac riverboat Company's boats. Water taxis run between National Harbor and Alexandria's dock behind the Torpedo Factory (at the bottom of Cameron Street) every thrifty minutes, between 10 a.m. and 10 p.m., with additional boats to meet demand for special events.

The Georgetown boat has a less rigid schedule, available on the Potomac Riverboat Company Website. As with all schedule or cost information, check in individual Web sites will provide current information, which may have changed since this publication went to press.

Christ Church

118 North Washington Street
www.historicchristchurch.org

Confederater Mass Grave and Christ Chuch
from Washington Street

In 1765, the vestry of the Chapel of Ease voted to replace the tiny chapel with another structure on the same site. John Alexander donated the land and John Carlyle commissioned James Wren to design Christ Church. To raise funds for the new structure, parishioners were taxed a certain amount of tobacco. Construction of Christ Church, the first Episcopal church in Alexandria, was briefly held up when funds ran out, but John Carlyle donated the remaining £220, and the church was turned over to the vestry on February 27, 1773.

The interior of the Georgian style church features a dramatic six-sided pulpit that appears almost to float before a Palladian window under a canopy suspended from the ceiling. Also in 1773, the architect (whether he was related to Christopher Wren is not documented) lettered the Lord's Prayer, the Apostles' Creed, and Golden Rule on the tablets that flank the three windows in the chancel, for an additional £8.

The Doric galleries were added in 1786, and the cut-glass chandelier under the galleries originally hung in the center of the ceiling when the vestry purchased it from England in 1817 for $140.

Located at what was then the upper end of Cameron Street, blocks from the busy center of town, the Georgian style Episcopal Church, which contemporaries referred to as the "Church in the Woods," has served its worshippers without interruption since its consecration.

Christit Church

George Washington was a vestryman. The families of General Washington and Robert E. Lee worshiped here regularly. Plaques identify their family pews near the front of the north side of church.

When Martha Washington died, Christ Church received the Washington family bible.

Nearly 400 unmarked graves, almost half of which were for children, date from 1787 to 1796, and some grave markers date from 1751. Officials estimate an additional 540 unmarked graves for years for which burial records are missing.

Other than the grave of unknown confederate soldiers just inside the Washington Street fence, the graveyard has not been used for burials since 1809, .

On January 1, 1942, President Franklin D. Roosevelt and Sir Winston Churchill attended services here on the World Day of Prayer for Peace.

Today, Christ Church is an active parish of over 2400 communicants

Open to the public for docent-led tours 9 a.m. - 4 p.m. Monday - Saturday and 2 - 4 p.m. on Sunday unless a wedding or funeral is in progress. The refurbished parish house contains a gift shop and small history museum.

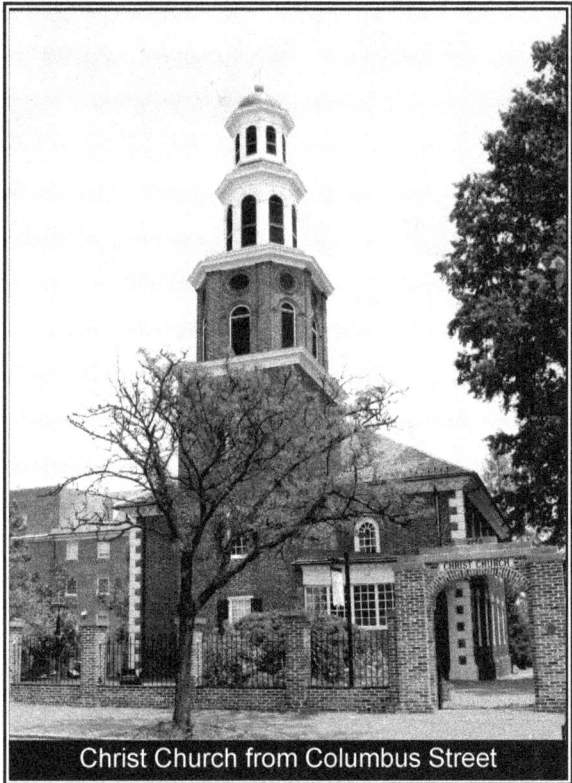

Christ Church from Columbus Street

George Washington Masonic National Temple

(Across from King Street's Union Station)
www.gwmemorial.org

The magnificent George Washington Masonic Memorial is a perfect example of being hidden in plain sight. The most visible landmark for visitors arriving in Alexandria, not only is it aesthetically interesting, but it also displays unique and irreplaceable historic artifacts, serves as a venue for concerts and community events and helps to demystify the beliefs of Freemasonry.

George Washington was the charter Worshipful Master of Alexandria Lodge No. 22, which upon his death, changed its name to Alexandria-Washington Lodge 22.

From the beginning of the 19th century, Lodge No. 22 met in quarters in Market Square. When those quarters burned, destroying many historic relics, it occupied new quarters within City Hall.

In 1945, the Lodge moved to the recently completed George Washington Masonic Memorial, known locally as the Masonic Temple.

Between visiting Christ Church and Friendship Firehouse, catch the King Street Trolley (page 9) to visit one of Alexandria's best kept secrets (and a "National Treasure").

The replica room in the southeast corner of the main floor, off Memorial Hall, is often overlooked because it is not included in guided tours. In addition to the original furniture and paintings arranged as they were in Lodge 22 in 1812, it displays the silver trowel the General used to lay the cornerstone of the U.S. Capitol, the Masonic apron embroidered for him by Lafayette's wife, and the bedroom clock that doctor and close friend James Craik stopped at the moment of Washington's death.

Masonic Temple (cont.)

The Replica Room

*M*emorial Hall contains a 17-foot bronze statue of Washington in Masonic regalia he wore to lay the cornerstone for the U.S. Capitol. A mural commemorating that event covers the south wall, and one depicting Masons attending a St. John's Day service at Christ's Church in Philadelphia (St. John is the patron saint of Mason's.) adorns the north wall. Stained glass windows featuring historic figures including Dr. Elisha Cullen Dick and General Lafayette, high in the walls filter the light that enters this impressive hall.

The George Washington Masonic National Memorial is the only Masonic building supported and maintained by the 52 Grand Lodges of the United States. Its mission is to educate and promote the virtues, character and vision of George Washington. The Memorial includes an array of surprises including a remarkable reproduction of the Ark of the Covenant, the handcuffs (at right) that John Brown wore to his execution, and the spurs that General Santa Anna was wearing when he was captured by Sam Houston.

The guided tours take elevators (at a 7 degree angle of ascent) to the ninth floor observation tower for a spectacular view of Alexandria and the waterfront. Washington monuments are visible to the north.

Descending from the observation platform, the elevator stops at each six additional levels, with exhibits that explain the origin, history and symbolism of the Masons.

The first floor offers a brief film about the history of Shriners in the United States, a 20-foot mechanized Shriner's parade and displays describing the work of Shriners' hospitals for children throughout the world.

The Memorial's excellent Web site (www.gwmemorial.org) provides additional information.

The Memorial is open from 10 a.m. – 4 p.m. daily, ex major holidays. Guided Tower Tours at 10:00 a.m., 11:30 a.m., 1:30 p.m. and 3:00 p.m.

The handcuffs John Brown' Wore to his execution

Friendship Firehouse

107 South Alfred Street

*T*he Friendship Fire House is easy to find, just look for the fireman weather vane. Friendship Fire Company, Alexandria's first volunteer fire company, was established in 1774. The current building, constructed in 1855 and later remodeled and renovated, replaces one that was destroyed—by fire—that same year. The fire house contains historic photographs, exhibits and antique fire equipment, including leather buckets and hand-drawn fire engines, with a nineteenth century meeting room on the second floor.

As you walk around town, notice the fire company marks on many of the old homes. These marks showed firefighters that the house is insured and with which fire company. A rival fire company arriving on the scene would not attempt to fight a fire in a house insured by another company.

According to undocumented tradition, George Washington was a founder and donated the first fire engine. Whether he slept here is not recorded (and unlikely).

The company became as well-known for its social and ceremonial functions as for fire-fighting.

Open Fri—Sat 10—4 and Sunday 1–4.

Brief tours (on request)last about twenty minutes.

The Lyceum:
Alexandria's History Museum

201 South Washington Street
www.alexandrihistory.org

Although his name is not as well known as George Washington or Robert E. Lee, Quaker Benjamin Hallowell, was another Alexandrian who made significant contributions to the city. A brilliant mathematician, Hallowell taught at a boarding school he established at 609 Oronoco Street that once had been the home of Robert E. Lee's cousin Anne and her husband John Wise, who owned Wise's and Gadsby's taverns. Hallowell also tutored the young Robert E. Lee, who lived next door at 607 Oronoco, when he was preparing to enter West Point. Lee had attended Alexandria Academy, which was founded by George Washington.

Hallowell established a scholarly society called the Alexandria Lyceum, which met at the boarding school from 1864 until he built the Greek revival building at 201 South Washington Street to

house the Alexandria Library Company (which had been established at the end of the eighteenth century) and to provide space for lectures, discussion and reading.

During the War Between the States, the Union troops occupying Alexandria commandeered the building as another of the 30 or so hospitals in the city. After the war, the Lyceum was used as a private home, an office building and the country's first Bicentennial Center.

Since 1985, Alexandria has used the building as its history museum, including Civil War documents and photos, and it is available for rent for special events, exhibitions and performances.

"Appomattox"
Duke and Washington streets

As Colonel Ellsworth (page 27) and a total of ten thousand Union troops took possession of Alexandria on May 24, 1861, the 800 Confederate troops who had been left to defend the city were gathering at the intersection of Prince and South Washington streets, two blocks west and one south of Marshall House.

The Alexandria garrison marched about three miles west along Duke Street to the Edsall Road station, to take the Orange and Alexandria Railroad to join the 17th Virginia Infantry at Manassas Junction. Alexandria remained in Union hands for the next four years, so the Confederate recruits would not return to Alexandria until the end of the war.

The statue is modeled on a melancholy soldier in John A. Elder's painting "Appomattox," which depicts General Robert E. Lee's surrender on April 9, 1865.

Virginia Governor Fitzhugh Lee, Robert E. Lee's nephew and a former major general in the Army of Northern Virginia, and General Joseph E. Johnston, commander of the Confederate Army of Tennessee, delivered dedicatory addresses on May 24, 1889.

Legislation passed by the Virginia House of Delegates in 1890, provided that permission to erect the statue "shall not be repealed, revoked, altered, modified, or changed by any future Council or other municipal power or authority," but the statue has roiled controversy among those who would have it removed.

The names of 100 of the Alexandria soldiers who did not return are listed on the pedestal, with the reminder that, right or wrong, "They died in the consciousness of duty faithfully performed."

The name of James W. Jackson, the innkeeper who killed Colonel Ellsworth at Marshall House was added to the east side of the statue in 1900.

The Dulany House

601 Duke Street

*W*hen he came to Alexandria in 1824, the Marquis de Lafayette addressed the crowd that gathered to greet him from the steps of the home of Benjamin Dulany, across Duke Street from the home in which he was staying, at 301 South St. Asaph.

Tradition also has it that Washington gave away "Miss French" who had been his ward, to Ben Dulany, his great friend when they married. The Dulanys were frequent dinner guests at Mount Vernon. Despite being a Tory, Dulany gave Blueskin, his favorite horse, to General Washington for his personal use during the Revolution.

Dulany, who joined Washington in laying the cornerstone of the U.S. Capitol in 1793, built the Duke Street house after the war.

Lafayette House

301 South St. Asaph

*T*he Marquis de Lafayette stayed here for a month in 1824. Congress commissioned the nineteen-year-old Lafayette major general July 31, 1777. He met Washington the next day. His son, George Washington Montier de Lafayette, lived with the Washingtons at Mount Vernon for five years while his father was in prison during the French Revolution.

On his last visit to the city, Lafayette offered a toast to Alexandria: "May her prosperity and happiness more and more realize the fondest wishes of our venerated Washington."

Nelly and Laurence Lewis lived here in 1831. Nelly Custis, who had been raised by her grandparents, George and Martha Washington, married Laurence Lewis, George Washington's nephew, at Mount Vernon on Washington's last birthday, February 22, 1799.

Marshall House

King and South Pitt streets

Elmer Ellsowrth had been a close friend of Abraham since working in his law office in Illinois. On May 2, 1861, the day after Alexandria voted to join the rest of Virginia in secession three river steamers carrying the 21-year old colonel and his Zouave regiment landed at the docks at the bottom of King Street in Alexandria. Ellsworth divided

his men into two squads, one to seize the railroads, the second, under his command, to capture the telegraph office.

As Ellsworth and his men crested the King Street rise at Fairfax Street, he saw an oversized Confederate flag flying from the roof of the Marshall House Hotel. The hotel, managed by an ardent and defiant secessionist named James W. Jackson, stood at the southwest corner of King and Pitt,

a block west of City Hall. According Edward House, a New York Tribune reporter, Ellsworth turned to his troops and said, "Boys, we must have that flag."

Ellsworth and seven men went to the hotel, bounded up the stairs to the top floor and climbed a ladder to the roof. Borrowing a knife from one of his men, Ellsworth cut down the flag, which he was rolling as he and his soldiers descended the staircase, with Private Francis Brownell in the lead.

As Brownell reached the first landing, Jackson stepped from the shadows with a double barrel shotgun aimed at Ellsworth's chest.

Brownell lunged for Jackson, attempting to deflect the weapon with his own, but Jackson fired, striking Ellsworth in the heart. Jackson's second shot went wild, piercing the wall of one of the rooms. Ellsworth's body fell heavily forward on the landing and Jackson reeled back as Brownell shot him full in the face, killing him immediately. Before Jackson's body hit the floor, Brownell ran him through with his saber bayonet with sufficient force to propel Jackson down the second flight of stairs, where he lay face down on the next landing.

Marshall House Hotel

But it was too late for Ellsworth, the first Union casualty of the war, and Jackson, the first Confederate martyr, as each lay face down, bleeding into the carpet.

President Lincoln burst into tears at the death of his beloved friend and ordered that Colonel Ellsworth's remains lay in state in the White House before being returned to New York for burial. Ellsworth's death became a rallying cry that brought thousands of new recruits to "Remember Ellsworth."

For his actions, Brownell received the Medal of Honor, the first awarded in the War Between the States.

The Hotel Monaco now stands on the site of Marshall House. A

Col. Ellsworth

plaque on the exterior wall to the right of the entrance, close to Pitt Street, memorializes the events of that day.

Stabler-Leadbeater Apothecary

105-107 South Fairfax Street
www.apothecarymuseum.org

When Edward Stabler founded the apothecary shop at 105—107 South Fairfax Street in 1792, Alexandria boasted about 300 houses. The shop served such famous citizens as the George Washington family, James Monroe and Col. Robert E. Lee. A plaque marks where Robert E. Lee was standing when Lt. J.E.B. Stuart told him that he had been ordered to quell the uprising at Harper's Ferry, October 17, 1861.

Stabler-Leadbeater   c. 1940

From 1792-1933, first the Stablers and then their son-in-law operated the pharmaceutical (cont.)

Stabler-Leadbeater (cont.)

company that in its heyday of manufacturing and sales occupied the entire block. Exposed brick visible at the bottom of shelves in the north wall of the gift shop at 105 limns where a doorway once opened to 103. It is one of many neat touches that allow visitors to feel the history of the shop.

Edward Stabler, an itinerant Quaker preacher and ardent abolitionist purchased slaves in order to free them. When he died in 1831, son William took over the business.

When William died in 1852, the business passed to Edward's son-in-law John Leadbeater, husband to the eldest of Mr. Stabler's sixteen children from two marriages.

During the War Between the States, the Apothecary shop was threatened when the Quaker owner refused on principle to sign a loyalty oath, swearing allegiance to the Union, which occupied the city throughout the war. The owners prevailed when a local judge — and long-time customer — vouched for Mr. Leadbeater.

The Civil War created new needs for medicines — Alexandria alone had 30 military hospitals — and the apothecary thrived, but after the war the business was in trouble.

When the shop closed in 1933, the owner simply locked the doors, leaving a rich trove of merchandise, equipment, ingredients and documents for posterity.

Most of the buildings' architectural features are original, and although the museum shop, in what had been the manufacturing side of the apothecary, has the bright lights and dashing design of countless other museum shops, crossing the threshold into the store, with original bottles and glass fronted cases, is about the closest to stepping into history a visitor is likely to come.

The jars on the shelves are the original jars that were on the original shelves. The fragile glass cases, the same.

Since 1982, the Stabler-Leadbeater Museum has been listed on the National Register of Historic Places.

Freedom House

1315 Duke Street
www.nvul.org

sales in the drawing room of the building. At their peak, the dealers sold as many as 1,800 slaves a year.

In 1836, Franklin and Armfield sold the slave compound that filled the 1300 block of Duke Street. A succession of slave dealers occupied the site, selling thousands more into slavery, until Union troops seized the city in May 1861.

Federal troops converted the slave pen to a jail, which purpose it served until it was again converted to use as L'Ouverture General Hospital for sick and injured black soldiers in 1864.

From 1875 -1885, it housed the Alexandria Hospital.

Local businessman Thomas Swann tore down the slave pens when he purchased the property in 1869.

From the mid 1880s until 1978, the building served as a boarding house or hotel.

In 1978 it was named a National Historic Landmark.

Renamed Freedom House in the 1980s, the building was dedi-

*I*n a twist worthy of Guy de Maupassant, the Freedom House Museum, commemorating slavery is in the basement at 1315 Duke Street, once headquarters the most prosperous and successful slave dealers of the nineteenth century, now headquarters of the Northern Virginia Urban League.

Isaac Franklin and John Armfield first leased the structure in 1828. Armfield negotiated his slave

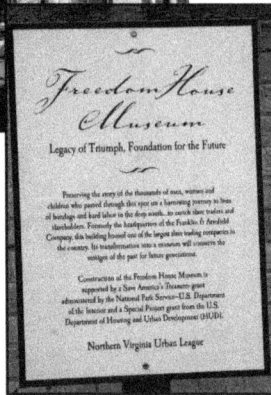

Getting there: From the King Street trolley, walk two blocks south on S. West or S. Payne to the 1300 block of Duke Street.

Freedom House

cated to the memory of the Reverend Lewis Henry Bailey who had been sold into slavery from the site and found his way back to Alexandria on foot. The Reverend Mr. Bailey founded several schools and churches, some of which remain.

In 2006, the Urban League, which had bought the property, began planning a memorial exhibition for the small basement of the structure, which had housed 60-80 men at a time, waiting to be sold down the river to the cotton fields of Mississippi and Louisiana.

The Urban League rededicated Freedom House on Lincoln's Birthday in 2008 and the new museum exhibits commemorating that period.

"We want people to know and feel the sadness of the horrific past... in this building," said Urban League president and CEO Lavern Chatman. "We want people to see that hope still existed [and] I want our kids to understand that that's where they come from."

"This isn't just a museum to see. This is where it happened.... We really want you to *feel*."

The Freedom House Museum at 1350 Duke Street in Alexandria is open Monday through Friday from 9 a.m. until 5 p.m. There is no admission charge, but donations are welcome.

Telephone 703-836-2858.

Freedmen's Cemetery and Soldiers Cemetery

E 131
FRANKLIN AND ARMFIELD
SLAVE OFFICE (1315 Duke Street)

Isaac Franklin and John Armfield leased this brick building with access to the wharves and docks in 1828 as a holding pen for enslaved people being shipped from Northern Virginia to Louisiana. They purchased the building and three lots in 1832. From this location Armfield bought bondspeople at low prices and shipped them south to his partner Franklin, in Natchez, Mississippi, and New Orleans, Louisiana, to be sold at higher prices. By the 1830s they often sold 1,000 people annually, operating as one of the largest slave-trading companies in the United States until 1836. Slave traders continuously owned the property until 1861.

DEPARTMENT OF HISTORIC RESOURCES, 2008

*T*he story of Freedom House is inextricably tied to the stories of Soldiers Cemetery, a few blocks south, and Freedmen's Cemetery a few blocks farther south and east.

From its inception, Alexandria's Freedmen's Cemetery—also known as the Contraband Burying Ground—has been different from most graveyards. Developed on land the Union confiscated from a Confederate sympathizer, the Freedmen's Cemetery was an active burial ground for only about five years. During that time, the African American graveyard was involved in a competition for bodies, at least one funeral hijacking and a protest by hundreds of wounded convalescents at the nearby L'Ouverture Hospital, in what is now the headquarters of the Northern Virginia Urban League and the Freedom House Museum.

African Americans—house servants, plantation slaves, and freed men—have been an integral element in Alexandria's development since the city was founded. In the eighteenth century, slaves cultivated the land and helped to construct the earliest buildings. By the end of that century, Alexandria had a substantial population of freedmen, many of whom had been manumitted as a cost-cutting measure by planters who had depleted the nutrients in the soil by planting the same crops—tobacco or wheat—every year.

By the nineteenth century, the price of domestic slaves had risen as international slave trade was banned and local slave owners could make a handsome profit by selling their slaves "down the river" to the great cotton plantations in the deep South. Alexandria became the center of that slave trade, and Franklin and Armfield, at 1315 Duke Street, were the most successful slave traders in the country, often selling more than a thousand slaves a year.

When Union troops seized Alexandria on May 24, 1861, they converted Franklin and Armfield's slave compound to a Federal jail. That same year, General William Butler, the commanding officer at Fort Monroe in Hampton, Virginia, made a landmark decision when he

Freedmen's Cemetery and Soldiers' Cemetery (cont.)

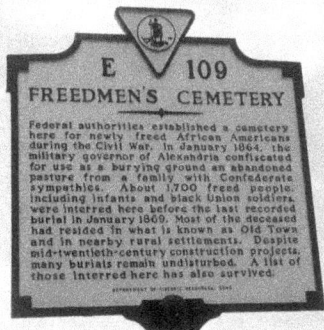

refused to return three escaped slaves who had made their way to the fort. Declaring that he was not obliged to return them because the Fugitive Slave Law applied only to domestic states and when Virginia seceded it became a foreign country. Therefore, Butler considered the escaped slaves to be contraband of war.

Like Fort Monroe, Alexandria remained in Union hands through-out the war, and like Fort Monroe, Alexandria saw a flood of escaped slaves seeking refuge. Destitute and ill-nourished, the refugees lived where they could, in abandoned buildings, government ("Contraband") barracks and hastily built shantytowns. Many of the refugees found employment in hospitals, in construction and other trades, as soldiers and sailors, and often as gravediggers.

In 1864, the Union jail was converted to L'Ouverture Hospital for African American and Native American soldiers. Named for Toussant L'Ouverture who led the rebellion to overthrow slavery in Haiti in the 1790s, (Hayti [sic] was a black neighborhood in Alexandria.) the 600-bed hospital was divided into 75-bed ward tents to provide ventilation and inhibit the spread of disease, according

Drummers at 2007 rededication of Freedmen's Cemetery

Freedmen's Cemetery and Soldiers' Cemetery

to the guidelines of the Quartermaster General.

In addition to casualties of war, infant mortality rates ran high, and smallpox and typhoid claimed the lives of thousands of Alexandria's African Americans, and the city needed a place to bury them. The city's Superintendent of Contrabands, an African American minister named Albert Gladwin, and Military Governor Brigadier General John P. Slough confiscated an undeveloped parcel of land at Church and South Washington streets from its pro-Confederate owner, a lawyer named Francis L. Smith. In late February 1864, the land began its life as the Contraband Burying Ground, a cemetery for African Americans.

Looking west to Soldiers' Cemetery

Entrance to Soldiers' Cemetery

Gladwin insisted that African American soldiers be buried in the Contraband Cemetery instead of the Soldiers' Military Cemetery, a few blocks from L'Ouverture Hospital, but African American troops in the town's hospitals insisted that they be buried with fellow soldiers in Soldiers' Cemetery. Captain J.G.C. Lee, the Assistant Depot Quartermaster at L'Ouverture, be-lieved that all deceased U.S. soldiers, including African Americans, were to be buried at Soldiers' Cemetery, also known as Alexandria National Cemetery, at the west end of Wilkes Street, about six blocks northwest of the Contraband Cemetery. Gladwin was insistent and obtained an order from the Military Governor, confirming that all black soldiers were to be buried in the Contraband Burying Ground, also known as the Freedmen's Cemetery.

Captain Lee disagreed, saying that soldiers must be buried on U.S. property, not a local burying ground. Besides, Slough had never officially directed him to bury the African American soldiers there.

Freedmen's Cemetery and Soldiers' Cemetery

Setting aside a separate area for black soldiers, Lee ordered that all soldiers be buried at Soldiers Cemetery'

Refusing to surrender, Gladwin arrested Lee's African American hearse driver as he carried the remains of an African American soldier to Alexandria National Cemetery. Sending the driver to jail, Gladwin redirected the funeral to Contraband, where the soldier was buried.

In December 1864, 443 soldiers recuperating at L'Ouverture petitioned to be buried along with their comrades in arms. "We are not contrabands, but soldiers of the U.S. Army," they said. They asked that their "bodies may find a resting place in the ground designated for the burial of the brave defenders of our countries [sic] flag."

Captain Lee appealed directly to General Slough, who said that he would abide by the decision of Quartermaster General, Major General M.C. Meigs, whose responsibilities included administering military hospitals. In December 1864, Captain Lee wrote his appeal to General Meigs, enclosing the petition from the African American soldiers at L'Ouverture. Apparently, Meigs agreed, because Gladwin was removed from his position and Lee resumed burying black and Indian soldiers in Soldiers' Cemetery.

Three Buffalo Soldiers graves at Soldiers' Cemetery.

In January 1865, the remains of about 220 black veterans were moved from Freedmen's Cemetery to the Alexandria National (Soldiers') Cemetery, where 37 regiments of U.S. Colored Troops (USCT) are interred at Alexandria National Cemetery, including five of the renowned Buffalo Soldiers.

A memorial plaque (on the large rock) marks the site where three soldiers who drowned in pursuit of John Wilkes Booth are buried in Alexandria National Cemetery.

Freedmen's Cemetery and Soldiers' Cemetery

When the war ended the Freedmen's Bureau assumed responsibility for the Contraband Burying Ground, but when President Andrew Jackson disbanded it in December 1869, the cemetery was closed and its previous owner, Francis Smith, reclaimed the land, which contained about 1,800 graves, more than half of them women and children.

Over the years, the wood grave markers rotted away. Unlike Soldiers' Cemetery, the whitewashed boards were not replaced with permanent grave stones.

In the early twentieth century, the Smith family conveyed the property to the Catholic Diocese of Richmond, which later sold the land, rezoned for commercial use. A gas station was erected on the site in 1955 and an office building in the 1960s.

The cemetery was forgotten until 1987, when city historian T. Michael Miller discovered an old newspaper article that alluded to a graveyard on the site. In 1994, Gladwin's burial log was discovered in the Virginia Library.

In 2007 the gas station and office building were razed. While examining the site, city archaeologists discovered evidence that the cemetery had been established on a prehistoric site. As they found evidence that they had discovered a grave shaft, they moved on, leaving the grave undisturbed.

In May 2007, the Freedmen's Cemetery was rededicated. Although it is now only a barren field, the Friends of Freedmen's Cemetery have begun planning a commemorative park on the site. For more visit :
http://www3.alexandriava.gov/freedmens.

Alexandria's National Cemetery predates Arlington's

African American Heritage Park

Holland Lane, south of 1700 Duke street

*A*cross Hoofe's Run from Alexandria National Cemetery, visitors can stroll through the eight-acre African American Heritage Park, which opened in 1995. Those unable or unwilling to walk on water or climb through a gap in the fence to the north will have to retrace their steps from the National Cemetery, walking a few blocks east and then cutting north to Jamieson Street. The African American Heritage Park is a block west between Hoofe's Run and Holland Lane.

The park boasts several sculptures by Jerome Meadows, an African-American artist who lives in the District of Columbia. The most prominent sculpture is a cluster of bronze trees called "Truths That Rise from the Roots Remembered," a tribute to African-American contributions to Alexandria's development. A sheltered book near the Roots sculpture provides background about Alexandria sites with special significance to African Americans. The antebellum Black Baptist Cemetery occupies an acre of the park, and a perimeter walk allows visitors to enjoy the wetlands that attract a variety of wildlife, from beavers to painted turtles.

"Truths That Rise from the Roots Remembered"

Alexandria Academy

604 Wolfe Street

tomb at Mount Vernon and the Lord Fairfax's house on Cameron Street (page 16).

In 1813, a freedman's association established a school for black children in a space that had been vacated by white children. Robert E. Lee studied here from 1818 to 1823, when trustees sold the building for use as a private residence.

During the War Between the States, the Union converted the building to use as a freedman's hospital. In 1884, the building was returned to the city and was used as a school and administrative offices until 1967. In 1995, Alexandria deeded the building to the Historic Alexandria Foundation.

*I*n 1785, a progressive group of Alexandria's leading citizens, including George Washington, founded the Alexandria Academy for Alexandria's children. In a letter to one of the other trustees, Washington stipulated that the private school would accommodate orphans, indigent children and girls ("not to exceed one girl for four boys") along with tuition students. Nephews George Steptoe Washington and Lawrence Washington attended, as did a number of black children. Washington contributed £50 every January until 1798, the year before he died.

The extant 1803 building was designed by William Yeaton, who also designed Washington's

In a letter to fellow trustees in 1786, General Washington wrote:

To the Trustees (Governors, or by whatsoever other name they may be designated) of the Academy in the Town of Alexandria, I give and bequeath, in Trust, four thousand dollars, or in other words twenty of the shares which I hold in the Bank of Alexandria, towards the support of a Free school established at, and annexed to, the said Academy; for the purpose of Educating such Orphan children, or the children of such other poor and indigent persons as are unable to accomplish it with their own means; and who, in the judgment of the Trustees of the said Seminary, are best entitled to the benefit of this donation. The aforesaid twenty shares I give & bequeath in perpetuity; the dividends only of which are to be drawn for, and applied by the said Trustees for the time being, for the uses above mentioned; the stock to remain entire and untouched; unless indications of a failure of the said Bank should be so apparent, or a discontinuance thereof should render a removal of this fund necessary; in either of these cases, the amount of the Stock here devised, is to be vested in some other Bank or public Institution, whereby the interest may with regularity & certainty be drawn, and applied as above. And to prevent misconception, my meaning is, and is hereby declared to be, that these twenty shares are in lieu of, and not in addition to, the thousand pounds given by a missive letter some years ago; in consequence whereof an annuity of fifty pounds has since been paid towards the support of this Institution.

Alexandria, Virginia: Where History Lives
ISBN-978-0-9826749-0-1

www.ingramcontent.com/pod-product-compliance
Lightning Source LLC
Chambersburg PA
CBHW031618040426

42452CB00006B/575